Praise for *Yardstick of Life*

"M. Shahid Alam's poems charm through their wit, and satisfy through their insights into the paradoxes of the human condition. The influence of the Urdu and Persian literary traditions is most apparent, but other influences make themselves felt as well, including—perhaps surprisingly—the language-molding of René Char and the plainspoken domesticity of William Carlos Williams. These lively poems of love, socio-political critique, nature, and the spirit reward the reader again and again."

—Luke Hankins, author of *Radiant Obstacles*

'The title of Shahid Alam's collection, *Yardstick of Life*, identifies a major focus of his work, a rigorous concern with measurement in several senses: the ways we measure—and judge or evaluate—life; the way life measures—and judges or evaluates—us (taking our measure); and the ways in which poetry itself, as a measured toolkit or a toolkit of measures, participates in those activities, not least by means of the author's careful calculation of poetry's capacities and limits.'

—Guy Rotella, author of *Critical Essays on James Merrill*

Yardstick of Life
And Other Poems

for editors of Kenyon Review

M Shahid Alam

May 2024

M. Shahid Alam

With foreword by Guy Rotella

Yardstick of Life: And Other Poems

Copyright © 2024 by M. Shahid Alam
Preface copyright © 2024 by M. Shahid Alam
Foreword copyright © 2024 by M. Shahid Alam

Other Books by M. Shahid Alam

Intimations of Ghalib (Orison Books, 2018)
Israeli Exceptionalism (Palgrave Macmillan, 2009)
Poverty from the Wealth of Nations (St. Martin's Press, 2000)
Challenging the New Orientalism (IPI, 2006)
Governments & Markets in Economic Development Strategies
    (Praeger, 1989)

Junaid

She asks the Lord of life
If he grants life in him

Acknowledgments

Guy Rotella

As a poet moonlighting in the department of economics, I rarely got to meet other poets. This changed in 2013 when I met Guy Rotella, Professor of English literature, at a meeting of one of the College committees. On learning that Guy is also a poet, I decided that I had to get to know him. I began by emailing him two of my English versions of Ghalib's ghazal. I got lucky. Guy had read Aijaz Ahmad's *Ghazals of Ghalib* (1970), a centennial celebration of the poet that contained English versions of Ghalib's ghazals by several eminent American poets, including W. S. Merwin, Adrienne Rich and William Stafford. Graciously, a few days later Guy sent me his careful reading of my versions of Ghalib, sprinkled with acute observations and insights. At some point, he also began sharing a few of his poetic gems with me. Thus began a literary friendship that continues to this day. Unknowingly, we had replicated a mentoring tradition in Urdu poetry, in which a senior poet—the *Ustäd* in Urdu—took a younger poet—the *Shägird*—under his wing, and schooled him in the finer points of language and poetry. This is how good things sometimes happen in our lives, by chance.

Literary Journals

Over some 55 years, my poems have appeared in the following literary journals, web magazines and weekly magazines: *Beloit Poetry Journal, Black Bear Review, Boiler Journal, Booth, Cape Rock, Chicago Review, Cold Mountain Review, Counterpunch, Holiday, Kenyon Review Online, Michigan Quarterly Review, New Letters, Nimrod, North American Review, Notre Dame Review, Paintbrush, Potomac Review, Prairie Schooner, Raritan, Salamander, Southern Review, TriQuarterly Online, West Coast Review, Western Humanities Review*. I would like to thank the editors of these journals for making my poetry available to their readers.

I have never seen anything without seeing God
nearer to me than it.

❖

I was a hidden treasure and wished to be known;
thus I created the world.

❖

Three thing from your world were made beloved
for me: women, perfume and prayer.

❖

If the hour comes upon you when you are planting
a date sapling, finish planting it.

The Prophet

Contents

    Title
    Copyright
    Dedication
    Acknowledgments
    Epigraph
    Contents
    Preface
    Foreword

1. Poems
3. Greek π
4. Apple
5. Goldenrods
6. Mother
7. Uncommon Care
8. Mary
9. Gentle Coaxing
10. Sounds Of Summer
11. Lark At My Window
12. Start In Life
13. Yardstick of Life

14. Sins of Arose
15. That Way
16. Circe
17. Genghis Khan
18. America's Past
19. Holding The Center
20. Macaques
21. Thanks
22. Birthday
23. Nirvana
24. Alone
25. Last Journey
27. Love Song in Eight Parts
37. Ten Ghazals
49. Six Days Of Spring
57. Pain
58. Gaia
59. Walk
60. Moth
61. Unseen
62. Archetypes
63. Bird of Paradise

64 Recite
65 Translation
66 Jesus
67 Veil
69 Dewdrops
81 Three Ghazals
87 About the Author

Preface

"For the saints…it is revealed that secondary causes are no more than 'veils' that keep people from seeing and knowing the Causer. It is like someone speaking from behind a screen and people thinking that the screen itself is talking."

Rumi

It is a bit odd that a poet should publish his first book of poetry at so advanced an age. Yes, I am 76. Arguably, it isn't good etiquette for a poet to be alive at this age.

Stranger still, this book contains poems written in my late teens and seventies, and the years between. Surely, this would result in a rather motley bunch of poems. To make matters worse, I do not attach a date tag to the poems.

In this I follow the tradition of the ghazal. In his *divan* (collection of ghazals) the poet does not arrange his ghazals by date of composition. Instead, he arranges them alphabetically using the last letter of their refrain (*radeef*).

This venerable poetic tradition insists that a ghazal stand on its own with no connection to the ghazals that precede or follow it. Indeed, each *sh'er* (distich) in a ghazal too is expected to stand on its own; nearly always, it is a poem in itself.

A *sh'er* distils some aspect of life, creation, a situation in love, a turn in our relationships, or one of the infinite colors of our feelings: and it has only two lines in which to do this. It is this pithiness of a *sh'er* that sometimes etches it in our memory. Therefore, in gatherings still connected to the ghazal, a writer or speaker will readily turn to a *sh'er* to brighten a conversation and embellish life itself.

Why then is this book of poetry so slim? Is this all the poetry I could produce in some sixty years of living?

Yes, this *is* all the poetry that life has permitted me. It is when we are afraid of losing our most precious moments that we want to turn them into poetry. Such moments are few; they are also fleeting and vanish before we can reach pen and paper.

I might have included another fifty poems if I had not destroyed them; but I will save for my memoir the true story of how I lost a third or more of my poems.

At the same time, I take comfort in the slightness of my poetic oeuvre for another reason. I do not wish to carry too heavy a codex of my own works during my travels in the afterlife.

A few days back when I cut open a papaya I marveled at the excess of seeds it contained at its core. What lovely, black, shiny pearls they were. If all these seeds could germinate, grow and bear fruits, some significant portion of the world's warm, rain-soaked lands would be covered in papaya trees.

Cut at the correct degree of ripeness, a papaya has a gentle sweet taste. For sweetness and fragrance, however, a papaya offers no competition to the mango. Not any mango to be sure, but mangoes come in varieties for which a king might offer his crown.

At its core, a mango contains just one seed, tightly and

securely wrapped inside a leathery pod, but if you wish to propagate the tree that bears the most heavenly mangoes, you could do better than rely on their seeds. Trees that grow from mango seeds may not bear any fruit, and if they do, the mangoes may not inherit the sweetness and fragrance of its ancestor.

A gardener trained in cultivating legacy mangoes, therefore, grafts scions from the prized mango tree to mango saplings. This is how the taste and fragrance of the prized mango spreads, and keeps spreading from one tree to another, from one generation to another.

This is how the ineffable core of the Islamic spiritual tradition was transmitted from one person to another, from one chest to another, across territories and across centuries. This tradition persisted even after its canonical texts had been committed to writing on camel bones, parchment and paper. It persists but also weakens in transmission.

There are aspects of every tradition—Muslims call this *baraka*—that elude the written word.

A poet succeeds when God grants him words, just a few words, to say what cannot be said in words.

---

[1] I published a previous volume of poetry, *Intimations of Ghalib* (Orison Books, 2018), that consist of my English versions of selected ghazals from Ghalib.

Foreword

The title of Shahid Alam's collection, *Yardstick of Life*, identifies a major focus of his work, a rigorous concern with measurement in several senses: the ways we measure—and judge or evaluate—life; the way life measures—and judges or evaluates—us (taking our measure); and the ways in which poetry itself, as a measured toolkit or a toolkit of measures, participates in those activities, not least by means of the author's careful calculation of poetry's capacities and limits.

At times, the book's assessments are conclusively direct and confident. This is especially true of a trio of overtly political poems that expose the tricks by which rulers or nations reify their hegemony as if it were inevitable and natural. In one, Genghis Khan and a U.S. Secretary of State share a self-exonerating tactic; they justify violence as the unwanted but necessary cost of self-defense while eliding the hierarchical assumption that underlies their grim and grimy logic: some lives are worth more than others. In "America's Past," the historical and museum preservation of the artifacts of slaughtered or displaced indigenous peoples is depicted as actually burying (in "crypts" and "vaults") what it presumably displays, suggesting that the very keeping of records can be a form of appropriation and erasure. Another, "Holding the Center," shows how seemingly neutral maps operate as willful instruments of coercion and control, nicely conveying its dissident point in the phrase "the cavalry / Of cartographers."

For all their shared interest in measurement, many of

the poems of Alam's collection are less concerned with the sort of corrective certitude just described than with more elusive forms of precision, forms in which uncertainty, doubt, and interrogation play a significant and transformative role. This is in keeping with the mixtures of exactitude and mystery, even mysticism associated with, for instance, the concrete yet eerie mathematics of pi and prime numbers, concepts that are aptly invoked in the volume's opening poem and help to establish its fundamental approach. It is related as well to the oppositions and mergers of high seriousness and deflating comedy, of elaborate formal patterning and disjunctive surprise familiar in Urdu poetry, especially the ghazal. Alam first made his mark as a poet with his creative translations of Ghalib, published by Orison Books in 2018, and that great poet's influence is vital throughout this book. Familiar images from the Urdu poetic tradition (roses, literal and legendary birds, moths and candle flames) are rehearsed and reimagined in several poems, for instance. More generally, throughout *Yardstick of Life*, in poems literally labeled as or otherwise recalling ghazals, in encounters where religious faith is challenged by or overcomes doubt, in sequences of love songs that explore the vagaries of romantic success and failure, in all of these, strategies of measurement (chronicle, biography, memory, curation, observed likeness or echo) encounter the infinite variety of experience, its refusals of or escape from category and capture.

These intricate measurements are often expressed by technical devices, artfully deployed. Some are traditional: the patterns of rhyme, repetition, stanza shape, and concluding self-reference borrowed from the ghazal. Others are more modern or contemporary, including sleights of meaning enabled by typography or word processing. In "Thanks," for instance, two of the obstacles to lasting love, too much intensity and too little, are conflated by a printing ploy: "in(s)anities," combining excess passion (insanity) with passion's exhaustion (inanity). In another, words are run together or otherwise combined ("dawnawakeneddolphin"; "rose:lipped rose:browed rose: eyed") to present a unity of sensation, cognition, and being that language, with its categorical rules and restrictions (grammar, syntax, orthography, and punctuation), otherwise betrays. As these stratagems suggest, Alam is often concerned with revising ordinary measures, something he frequently accomplishes in poems treating the natural world and human interactions with it. One poem revises the standard term for bringing branches of flowering shrubs into early bloom ("forcing"), calling it "gentle coaxing" instead. Another uses the unpredictability of bird song to teach us to be wholly pleased by less than the full measure of a plenitude we too often forcefully insist on. In number VIII of a set of ten ghazals, loss, seemingly made inevitable by repetition, is nonetheless transformed into persistence. In one poem of the sequence called "Six Days of Spring," even sobriety and joy prove interchangeable.

Of all the subjects this book takes up, time, with its repertoire of life-narrowing threat (death) and life-enhancing expansiveness (the grace of living), is perhaps the most insistent and central (no surprise, since time is an abstract and relative thing we measure as it measures us). The book's varied reactions to time, ranging from despair to joy and including efforts both faithful and mistrusted to transcend it (see "Nirvana"), are among the collection's greatest pleasures. Other readers will find other things to admire. For me, the most moving moments in *Yardstick of Life* are those timeful, lasting ones that invoke the quiet mysteries of family life, and do so in ways that, to say it again, revise the conventional categories by which experience is usually meted out or measured. In one, a mother at prayer amid ordinary household tasks enacts the interpenetration of the eternal and the quotidian or commonplace, dissolving, at least momentarily, the standard conception of an unbridgeable gap between them. In another, a father learning to care for an infant son discovers that constraint can liberate rather than, as is usually thought, enslave, a discovery that transforms the child's demands into gifts and makes burdens pleasures. In such poems earthbound measurement expands to encompass the possibility of spirit.

Guy Rotella
Emeritus Professor of English Literature
Northeastern University, Boston

POEMS

Greek π

Walk like a Greek π.
    Your path lies inside you.

Become a prime number.
    Nothing can divide you.

She will delight (in) you
    After she leaves you.

Life does not happen
    Until it happens to you.

Suffer the scorpion:
    It dare not sting you.

Lucky you cannot be
    Until luck leaves you.

You have not lived:
    If death is not for you.

Apple

An apple falls from an apple
tree: the word when it hits
the ground is a soft thud. Who
is privy to this slice of life?
Who chronicles, saves it
in some cosmic cloud? Is there
a busy eye in the sky
archiving the biography
of an apple tree, a raindrop,
a bumblebee? Perhaps,
time's curator returns
this moment ad infinitum,
so that I will hear ages hence,
at exactly this mingling
of time and memory,
the same apple falling
from the same apple tree
with the same soft thud.

Goldenrods

Rows of goldenrods rise
  to brighten my day.
    Is their beauty
      not for me
        but for the bee?
        If nature crafts
         this splendor
          for the butterfly
        and bee, why
      does it deep stir
      the poet inside me?
    In the bee, beauty
   makes honey: in man
it becomes epiphany.

Mother

Evening elevates her.
Quiet, under night jasmines,
Not far from where the children
Shout at play, on an heirloom
Cashmere rug she prays.

She is herself this hour
A thing unknown. As dusk
Unfurls silken veils in the air, she
Is forgotten: as she too appears
To have forgotten us. Alone,
She is lost in one alone.

Amidst gently whispering leaves,
Stirred to life by monsoon breeze,
She returns: not the least changed
By her passage through eternity,
Ready as always to resume
Her common cares.

Uncommon Care

For my son, Junaid

For several months now,
I've scarcely slept or rested,
Watching a fresh-rigged sprite's
Passage to terrestrial life.
Answering this fledgling's
Demands for food, love
And song; waiting upon
Its cherubic motions;
Teaching give, take,
Wait, watch, listen,
Sleep, wake, grow.
This daily drudgery,
This loss of liberty
Has made me aware
Of an uncommon care
For soft-bellied sprites
Adapting to love and light.

Mary

For my son, Junaid

All day, she grieves for him,
For sunlit days unborn in him.

She tells her grief to stars.
She cancels spring for him.

In dreams, she starts her day
Still packing lunch for him.

She laughs to lift my grief.
She takes her cue from him.

She asks the Lord of life
If he grants life in him.

Cell morphing inside him,
God took her son to him.

Gentle Coaxing

with credits to Marcia Passos Duffy

You can force quince, lilac and spirea
Into an early spring. The trick
Is to cut off a branch with flower
Buds, split open the stem end
With scissors: if the stem is woody
Tap it with a mallet. Immerse
The lower end in a vase of warm
Water, leave it in a cool place, away
From sunlight: then wait for the buds
To bloom. You can force forsythia
To bloom in one to three weeks; cherries
Take longer. Lilacs are more stubborn:
They may take up to five weeks. In late
Winter, you can bring the look of spring
To your living room. Some gardeners
Call this craft – gentle coaxing.

Sounds Of Summer

Teams of mowers, trimmers
Scatter summer's buzz of bees.

Sorties of low-flying biplanes
Spread slander in the sky.

Bikers, rockers, rappers
Shred the silence of trees.

Summer sounds retreat.
Nature is switched to mute.

Lark At My Window

Lark at my window, go away.
It's not yet light. I timed my flight
For five: it's not yet midnight.

Lark at my window, go away.
You disturb my sleep.
Sing psalms to the night,
Madrigals to the moon,
Herald the roseate dawn.

Wake me at sunrise.
Tweet me for luck
When I reach for plenitude.

Start In Life

It is a woman's start in life
to keep the world waiting,
to slow down the clocks
till seconds move like hours,
till each seed becomes a tree,
till each drop goes out to sea,
till each man, lusty in his prime,
grows old from the gravity
of waiting, waiting for you.

Yardstick Of Life

Clasping the tenderest neck
Of my evening like clematis
Dying in rebirth, the very-lily
Of tenderness clasping the neck
Of my evening, the very tastebuds
Sweetening the humid beauty
Of my evening like labiate darkness
Since death is the very yardstick of life.
Like a flash of concentrated sleep,
Pass your hands over the swanneck
Elegance of death over-and-over
Unruffling slender-white swanneck
And what you feel is not her feathers
Against your translucence but your lyre
Against the very-neck of evening
For death is the very yardstick of life.

Sins Of aRose

What are the sins of aRose
My lilied sleep dawnawakeneddolphin
Rose of beauty rose of power
Rose of softeagernesses myRose
What a rose of dying tenderness
Deathless light in night's heart
Of darkness. Reach out myRose
To soft insinuating bliss of
Undethronededen, oysterheart crying
For rose:lipped rose:browed rose:eyed
Roundness of pearl. Let embalm myRose
In the yoga of perfumed out:going
And in:coming. Last dawnofthenight
In the morning's throatofdarkness
Rose from sleeping unawareness
From cloudy amor:phousness
From milky dewiness to redness
Raging in death's sweet innocence

That Way

In blindfold: she
likes *him* that way.
Foot-bound, he
likes *her* that way.
They in love: sure
it stays that way.

A musical hag
took him away.
She on a dragon
rose, swept away.
Life may, love never
stays that way.

Circe

Circe still keeps this isle,
    Though now for mere lucre.
      Men thrown here by rare
        Mischance, delight in her
      Incurably, interrogating her
    Icy flesh & marble bones
For shards of beauty.

Genghis Khan

I think this is a very hard choice, but the price,
we think the price is worth it.
Madeleine Albright

When Genghis Khan swept through
Samarkand, he did not shrink from
The hard choices. His men carried out
A general carnage, not sparing women
Or children. Afterwards, when Genghis
Inspected the mounds of dead bodies,
Skulls piled into pyramids, he knew
Instinctively (he had been trained for it)
That the price was worth it. Genghis
Did not revel in carnage: his shamans
Opposed it. But he had to answer to
Mongol mothers. If the piled-up skulls
In Samarkand produced fewer body bags
In Karakorum, the price was worth it.

America's Past

This great country, stretching from coast to coast,
Packed with cities, suburbs, missile silos, ball parks,
Dump sites, has preserved its past. The first explorers,
The first cohorts of settlers, ranchers, gun slingers,
Gold diggers, understood the debt they owed
Posterity. They carefully recorded everything
They did: the forests cleared, battles fought, Indians
Decimated: the buffalo, bobcat, moose, wolf, and fox
Hunted to near extinction: the rivers forded, dammed,
Polluted: the sacred mounds, ancient burial grounds
And villages ploughed under. All this history was saved
In diaries, travel books, novels, memoirs and letters
Still preserved in some forgotten attic. Soon the artists
Joined this historical project, traveling, capturing fast-
Fading images in charcoal, paint, wood, bronze and stone.
A late arrival, the box camera worked the last shift,
Gathering the last fading faces from the scroll of history.
Every city now displays – in crypts, vaults, and museums
Set aside for Indians and natural history – proud collections
From the past, still, excavated lives, scalps, feathers, barks,
Beads, bones, totems, pottery, mummies – all carefully
Catalogued, indexed, laminated, saved for posterity.

Holding The Center

I taped it to the wall, map of the world,
Rand McNally, printed in the USA.
It splits Asia right down the middle:
The truncated moieties exiled to the right
And left edges of earth made flat.
It was necessary, this sundering: so
USA could sit right spat
At the center of subjected memory.
It isn't easy holding the center,
Mind you. See to it
That they *see* you holding it.
You have to mobilize the cavalry
Of cartographers, the hired guns of history,
To center the world on you.

Macaques

Observe them in their forest habitat: their
Pedigree is older than our own. They
Eat what they can pick or pluck:
This keeps them limber, moving. Of
Leisure time, they have more than we do,
But none of our angst about what
To do with it. They groom each other
For companionship; at times, they groom
Other species too. After a midday nap,
The young males raid pantries
In nearby villages: but take few spoils
From the escapade. At night they seek out
Nested branches, to huddle together, soft,
Pillowed against the night's chill. They
Are up again at first light, rested, playful,
Eager to start another macaque day.

Thanks

My fifty years with you
feel like a day.

Good thing too.

It can be hard
making it through
the in(s)anities
of this maze.

Thanks
      for making it
                short
                        so easy.

Birthday

Happy birthday!

I fixed the light switch
inside the fridge.

Sorry, I took
so long to fix this.

I would not do it
on any ordinary day.

Nirvana

    Set against the clarity
     of a sky like this,
   time, flux and flow
are overcome:
  motion ceases,
    motion of karma,
      setting free the ego
        from mordant vanities.

Alone

Will you be alright?

What could I say?
Days later he
was gone.

His going
did not sink
until there was
no light left in him;
until the night left
him, alone,
with me
alone.

Will you be alright?

His words
wash over me
like acid
like ashes
like the sea.

Last Journey

Where are you going Sir?
 To Heaven.
We don't go there.
 We'll see.

At the last stop
medics in blue coats
carried a corpse
out of the train.

The train rested
on the tracks: it was
a star-bereft, late
winter night.

It was the train's
last journey.

Love Song
In Eight Parts

1

I

Just once
 the way
  you sat
   beside me
    brought to end
     my trembling
      at your alterity;
     the memory
    now of this
amazes me.

II

Gently, she
took off
the shoes
he died in.

In death, *he*
had more
felicity
than in life.

III

   Though I vary
  with the season's
 drift, and change
from sorrow
to sorrow:
 sea-girt or
  isle-bound,
   through wind,
    wave and hail,
     I keep reaching
      for, yet drifting
       away from you.

IV

    The rose in a mirror
  is never a rose.
Not so your rose
in me. See how
   you are memorialized,
      sung to, and surprised,
     by the searing light
        of love reviving me.

V

You are a cube of sugar.
Sweeten my cup of tea.

You are dark matter.
Bind me with gravity.

You are a field of dew.
Why am I thirsty?

Why fly out there?
Come nest inside me.

VI

The night exudes longing
In the languor of sighs.

One angry look removes
Many layers of disguise.

I open another skylight
When sleep seals your eyes.

VII

Without art or artifice,
  without proof or prefaces,
    without clock or calculus,
      without love's hocus-pocus,
        without chants, prayers, beads,
      without vows, marriage deeds,
    she settled into my abyss,
invisibly, by degrees.

VIII

This dough rises
  with love's leaven:
    this bubbling wine
      overflows life's cup:
        this song made
      flesh, this gift
    of love to life
enlarges us.

Ten Ghazals

I

He makes each day a resurrection.
Quran (25:47)

From sleep you awake
To mercy and his might.

He resurrects your body
To see *you* in his light.

Consider, why your days
Alternate with nights.

Sháhid, you were a clot.
Remember and recite.

II

You too would think the world of her
If you like *Qays* would look inside.

When Gabriel commanded, *Read*,
Muhammad froze and shook inside.

Muhammad brought the idols down.
Have you since then looked inside?

Sháhid, these pithy words are proof,
For ripeness you must cook inside.

Qays: archetype of distraught lover in Arabian legend;
Read – Iqra, in Arabic – the first words of the Qur'an
conveyed to Muhammad by Gabriel.

III

It gets harder staying true.
It has been touch and go.

Bye, he said and was gone.
And I, What a way to go.

Hew your tree into an ark.
Find your ocean, let it go.

How will you deal with us
If *he* lets your people go?

Sháhid, a sufi chided me,
You have a long way to go.

IV

You pledge your heart to joy.
I celebrate a night of pain.

Stay awake. Invisibly, *he*
Slips into your night of pain.

Do not leave yet. Share
With me this night of pain.

Sháhid, your days of joy
Are born in my night of pain.

V

The champaks have served the sentence of blight.
Their passion irrupts in an erotica of flowers.

The boys of basant unfurl their manhood in kites.
The city sky shimmers in a skirmish of colors.

I have watered a wilted sycamore day and night.
That sycamore has roots reaching into the air.

Will there be another night of pain so bright?
I will treasure all my days if death is so rare.

Basant (bus-unt): spring kite-flying festival in South Asia

VI

When the night overtakes starlings in flight,
I open my arms till they rest inside me.

Give me a vision of things as they are.
Clear days awaken this quest inside me.

When I see the strong batter the weak,
The blood of Hussein protests inside me.

The days of our love will never leave me.
You have come home. Nest inside me.

VII

If tulips are in bloom, what primal angst,
Whose love unspent quickens them to life?

If *his* time is not ours, can the infinite slip
Through the infinitely small eye of a needle?

Strike your mallet on the chisel. Some
One! Free the light raging inside me.

All our generations grew out the first.
There was no death till Adam knew Eve.

Life fights entropy, bad for love's business.
Dying brings back light. Death, stay out of it.

VIII

As night passes, birdsongs fill the air
Like fireworks the sky: then they are gone.

Aspens, oaks write their autumn odes
In tints of gold: then they are gone.

For a few years children transfix us
With their stories: then they are gone.

In tents of summer nights, I will recall
Love's scented days, what if they are gone.

IX

A swathe of periwinkle blue thriving in April;
this won't last till May.

A pair of waxwings warble outside my window;
they are real not painted.

Once-green, rain-sodden leaves hug the grass:
scenes from a massacre.

Light from distant galaxies varnishes the winter sky;
it is brighter than ochre.

X

No man is an island entire: you
Are one, becoming another.

Is this how we got smarter?
Eaten by one, eating another.

These are life's only chances.
God is one, dying another.

Sháhid, is this your luck in life?
Wasting one, wanting another.

Six Days
Of Spring

I

Again, the dogwoods, silver bells, magnolias and cherries
Dash to life and light in a florid swirl of colors: red, purple,
White and magenta twirls. It is the urge to procreate
So long suppressed that propels this playful excess.

This time of year nature shines brightest in flowers.
It understands what texture, pattern, color, scent
Will coax the bird, bee, beetle and butterfly
To bless each flower's tented bridal bed.

In leaves,
       the sober greens will speak
                       when April turns to May.

II

After a few days of New England's slow-leaving rain,
A glorious sun was out minting gold coins
So wafer thin they hovered in the air.
I took a handful and bought myself
A pint of joy. It lasted a few days.

III

In April, earth thanks
        the sun in flowers:
Starting with tulips,
        cheerful allegro:
Rising to magnolias,
        dreamy allegretto:
Crowned in daffodils,
        boisterous finale.
Only in late May, after
        crocus, tulip and lily,
Earth greets husband sun
        in gratifying greens.

IV

I knew it was Spring –
    when first I saw a clutch of tulips,
        break into flamenco dance. In
            a wink, time took the dancers
                back to summer's anteroom. Now
            the carnage of leaves has begun. Cold,
        worm-eaten, crated, shall I outlast
      time & winter snow's melting
for new wonders to begin?

V

Not two weeks back in May, I took you home.
Such tenderness I had not seen all winter.
Scent in the air, sun-light, what colors.

Past glory, you reveal new colors,
Sober green, secure. Where have I seen
Such staying power? Stay the summer with me.
Gather snow in winter. Carry me back to spring.

VI

It comes down, dropping
   like dew from the sky, tiny
      revelations, if only we knew
         the source from where they flow
        as mercy. I stepped out of my
       dark cavern of self-nesting
         into the blue-kenning sky
      of his presence. A skylark
     traces an arc across the sky
      on light wings, closing, spreading
     in his mercy. I had the wind
under my wings. I flew.

Pain

In burnished white last night
pain knocked on my door.
It had no shape I knew
of man or mythos: it was
neither beast nor deity.
Unasked, it entered &
whispered in my ear,
you will not sleep again
this side of death. Now
wide awake day & night
I cleave salt ranges of pain,
assaying all my chances
of taking God back to man.

Gaia

It's your
world
for now.

Keep it.
Debauch it.
Gouge it.

Stuff it
till your gut
explodes.

We will
be back
when you
go out.

Walk

Walk, there is God's mercy in it.
Muhammad

Walk through sandstorms of doubt.
Walk through gullies of despair.
Walk through gorges of pain.
Walk through nagging now.
Walk through nowhere.
Walk in prayer.
Walk to dare.
Walk on air.

Moth

Man is a moth, God a candle.
When mothwings wrap the flame,
Why should the waxwings not burn
And *it* perish in the flame? A moth
That shuns the flame's incandescence
Is not a moth. A flame that cannot
Draw the moth, that will not burn
It to ashes instantly - is not a flame.
A god that mind can know is not
God: it is man's alter ego.

Adapted from Rumi, *Fihi Ma Fiha*

Unseen

When the dark night of insurgence
Ended, what I saw I had not seen.
I saw the hills ascending, coruscating,
Singing in a million tongues of green.
I greeted colors by their singular names,
Azure, indigo, cerulean, aquamarine.
I understood why red is iridescent,
Why blue is boundless, serene?
I knew why earth dreams in colors,
Why night sky burns to be seen, why
Light enters the heart when the eye
Learns to see: it is itself unseen.

Archetypes

A river flows through him.
A rainforest grows inside him.
A mountain meditates with him.
Only the huma and hoopoe
Circling, only the Simurgh,
Know him. Only they
See him as he sees them,
Archetypes of heaven,
Shedding feathered light
On snow-peaked mountains,
Lilied valleys, wren-filled skies,
Bee-full hives, leaf-hauling ants,
Lissome cheetahs, schools of fish
Swimming inside oceans. A brush
From a single simurgh feather, unveils
Myriad tented beauties inside him.

Bird Of Paradise

Have you seen this splendor, this moon-washing night?
More pulsing than platonic, this night that dances
To the cadence in my heart, that comes to nest
Inside my breast, bird of paradise.

I have died on this surging night,
Death in breath out, more times than I
Can remember. Slight as feathers it arrives
Down the soul's skylight: it is dark: it is bright.

This night unveils the power of a thousand nights.
It enters on the wings of the silver simurgh,
Night in day out: it is my guest till dawn
Awakens a day cradling the sky.

This night is not a streaming of felicity
But its cessation: it is time staying the flow
Of time. It is time that tells no story; this time
Surpasses glory. It is time that does not know its name.

Recite

          Stepping out, everything I saw
    Was light, airy, recondite.
I saw no granite city, towered,
   Boxed, standing above me.
     What I saw was light, dappled
        Gold, bottle blue, myrtle green,
     Light bending, coruscating, fluid,
   Striated. There was light too
Traveling in circles, spiraling,
   Descending, ascendent, light
     Turning lucent, crystalline.
      There was light coming down
        In arabesques, filigreed silver,
      Winged silk, penciled gold. I saw
    Light engaging light, inviting,
Exclaiming, declaiming, *Recite*.

Translation

All poetry contains echoes
of Eve's first song. In slow
cadence it comes to us,
In poetic migrations,
played on flute & string.
Inside a poem listen
for the first lover's cry.
Inside a poem listen
for a child's first
chime of surprise.
All poetry translates
from buried scrolls, from
vanished hieroglyphs, from
the concerto of feelings
to the poetics of discovery.
Translation is not treachery.
It is not a poem if it forgets
the least bit of its history.

Jesus

At dawn tomorrow
Hired assassins at city gates
Will hunt down the infant Jesus.

Another unborn day will be stained
With the blood of flowers.

Another cri de coeur
Will end in despair.

Another era will seek
Plenitude in erasure.

Veil

Veil your awesome beauty.
Stretch it to a maximum; this
Sanctifies your power.

Easily the heads can turn.
Try (if you can) to animate
Dead ashes in an urn.

Stripped, you lose power.
Men toss the cold detritus
Of flesh sloughed by you.

Thread by thread unweave
Your mystery. In signs,
Reveal your source to me.

Dewdrops

Bare Trees

Slate blue clouds, bare trees
   Standing sentinel: in the air
      A mild chill. What a way,
God, to meet on this hill.

Heaven

Beyond dark clouds
  Heaven rises blue.
    You feel pure haiku
When rain washes you.

Frogs

Once again frogs in water-holes
   Croak their throaty mating songs: jarring
     No doubt to human ears but lusty
Baritone to females of their kind.

Amaryllis

Give me time to write
   A ruba'i to every amaryllis.
     After that, make one woman
Shine eternal in a ghazal.

Evening

The evening is like red wine
   Poured into clear glass. Time
    Puts his lips to the glass &
Slowly sips it to the last.

Cyan Blue

A January sky
  Shines the same
    As a sky in July.
      Both are cyan blue.

On Some Days

"They that day were nearer to unbelief than to belief…"
Qur'an: 3,167

On some days I am
nearer to unbelief
than to belief.

On other days
he pivots me around.

Do You

Affirm, I cry
Inside the heart's dark
Retreat: affirm that you
Exist. Sudden, a voice
Echoes, *Do you*?

Hearth

I light a fire
turning my heart
into a hearth. I wait
until this waiting
ends my time
on earth

Three Ghazals

I

My eyes are two distilleries. She
Snapped, I have no taste for tears.

Not I, my tears are shedding tears.
For I long since have died in tears.

Death's angel came to take me back.
Grief-stricken, he too left in tears.

Shahid, stay a few more days. She
May come back to you in tears.

II

She asked me, Sir, what is life?
Let me live and love, my life.

A song, I said, from ruby lips.
She said, Do I not love your life?

She said, Go, you love with lips.
By your lips, I love with life.

Shahid, when the lilies bloom,
Seize all chances: this is your life.

III

We live the life that could not be.
And I am what I could not be.

In hopes of life, in fear of death,
This life is what life could not be.

Wanting many, we only live one.
All the rest what could not be.

Shahid, your life is what it had to be.
Never mind what could not be.

About the Author

M. Shahid Alam began his life in Kolkata, was born in Dhaka in September 1947, where he lived until April 1971. Since then he has lived in Karachi, Bloomington, USA, London, Canada, again in Karachi, Kingston and Montreal, Canada, Hamilton, New York, and Boston and North Attleboro, Massachusetts.

He moved to Massachusetts in September 1988. Apart for a sabbatical year in Karachi, he never moved again. Measured in terms of life experiences excluding the time spent with his family—he has lived nearly all his life in Dhaka and Karachi. All his working life was spent at various universities, except for four months working as a reporter for *Outlook*, a political weekly based in Karachi. He could wish it had been the other way round.

Where you live matters if you are accumulating memories that matter. The people who mattered most in his life—prophets, sufis, poets, philosophers, historians, scholars, composers, and singers—were always willing to move with him, no matter where he went. What luck: what a life.

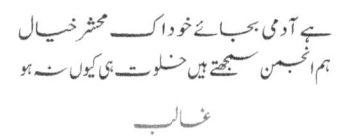

ہے آدمی بجائے خود اک محشر خیال
ہم انجمن سمجھتے ہیں خلوت ہی کیوں نہ ہو

غــالــب

Made in United States
North Haven, CT
22 March 2024